I0210812

On the Hard Edge of Hollywood

Scott Shaw

Buddha Rose Publications

First Edition 2002
Second Edition 2011

ISBN 10: 1-877792-38-1
ISBN 13: 978-1-877792-38-0

10 9 8 7 6 5 4 3 2 1

Printed in the United States of America

On the Hard Edge
of *Hollywood*

1

I guess it all started in '69
'69, moved from south-central L.A. to
hollywood
an apartment on harold way
     a dirty little side street
     off of hollywood and normandie
     lined with some 1960's
     style square apartment buildings
     some 1940's houses
     losing their lost way
     in the lost world
     of rapid change
I was eleven
the hippie *thAng* was full on
I'd walk down the boulevard and see
dudes
eyes *tripp'n* deep,
lost into the realms of some vision
unseen/unknown
     L-S-D
I'd walk the streets because
there was really nothing better to do
the deep hot summer, full on
AM radio blasting pop rock n' roll
new kid on a kid-less street
no one to talk to
except the old dreamers
with no passion left to feel
too old to know
that it was too late
too late to be left alive

eleven years old
I walked among them
the hippies and the old poets
seeking a reason/my reason
dreaming of all the things
a 1969 kid dreams about
but, instead I was handed:
white cross, jones, and acid
never dreaming I'd live so long
to be smashing hard into the realms of
the
one of them
the too longed lived
but, here I am twenty-five plus years
later
running from hollywood
but, hollywood chases me
hollywood is never too far away

2

music pounds hard
rhythmic movement
I got a drink in my hand
but, the music
it makes me want to dance

red light
dead center, pouring into my eyes
it almost blinds my sight
like a camera flash/like the sun

passing in front of it
moving as if moving meant something
      the red light
      it momentarily
      is blocked

I see the vision
the vision is clear
her form
      an ancient dance
slithering like a snake about to strike
a python, ready to kill

a chrome bar, passes up to the ceiling
a chrome bar
like a fireman would slide down
she, she moves up to it
wraps her legs around it
making love to it/she embraces it

spinning into a sexual frenzy
on a chrome pole
        hard, very hard
        steel hard
        hard
        like no real man
        could ever stay

in her spinning
her eyes meet mine

she slides down
down off of the pole

movement
her body lays down on the floor
she spreads her legs
her pelvis raises up
down/up/down/up
she fucks the air

I pull a dollar bill out of my pocket
I put a dollar bill into my mouth
I walk up to the stage
eye to eye
I slowly remove it from my lips
sliding it from side to side
I lick it
I lay it on the bars surrounding her

bars to keep me out
bars to keep her in
I don't know
she smiles/I smile
a dollar spent
a dance done
it all means nothing

another dollar
on a promises illusion
which will never happen

3

the lights smash down hard
on the drunken head
of a drunken man
attempting to find mysticism
in the hands of lust
at the hands of excess

surrounded by fools
the fools of the world
who drink only to drink
heredity/psychology/escape

       but, escape to where?
       I've always pondered
       escape to why?
       the question remains

a seedy club
on the wrong side of hollywood
they pour their watered down beer
out of the tap/into a glass
a promised illusion of nothingness

I sit among them/the fools
fools like me
we all have our reasons for being here
the reasons all equal the same thing

nothing

4

night time—promised passion
the pacifier of dreams
we, venchenzo and me, sit
in a semi sleazy hollywood bar

smalls

a little place over on the non-fag side
of santa monica boulevard

it's almost christmas
they've strung a bunch of christmas
tree lights
across the ceiling

     it's very bright in here
        very light
     when it is usually very dark

     very light
     too much to be seen
     in a room with not
     too much worth looking at

we got here early
we got one of the two booths

we sit back
my back leans against the brick wall
we continue the wetting of our lips

     drink

we smoke some cuban cigars
seeking a vision
worth visualizing
in a bar-room filling
with the too old to know any better
the too young that still think this place
is cool

and, I guess I just never learned the
rules
too restless to ever really care

and, I guess they say jesus is a savior
but, you can't be saved
when you just don't believe

so, here I sit
across the table from venchenzo
one of the...
no, two of the damned

two, who just never cared enough to
care
two, who never attempted to believe the
lie

we sit
we watch

we laugh at the joke engulfing our
presence
people/saturday night
thinking they are/pretending they are

one of us
one of the damned

I look/I see
it is obvious they are not
they still believe

5

venchenzo and I go back
twenty, twenty-five years deep or so
another hollywood kid
with a mind full of dreams
and a world smashing down
way too hard
to ever dig his way out enough
to live any of them

him and me
two down *mutha' fuckers*
coming straight out of the ghetto
noth'n left to lose

he came up over by hollywood and
western
up the street from the *saint francis*
hotel
they've shot movies there
        junky/whores/murderers
        they all made it their home

they always shoot movies on our old
turf
some people even dream to live
on those dirty violent streets

        badlands in a bad world
            a fool's desire

        thus for, and as such

him and I
venchenzo and me
we go out
OUT
to lose our selves
deep into the night

      deep into the dark
            deep into the drink
and the various other forms of
intoxication

     seeking vision
         seeking solace
              seeking forgiveness

seeking something/anything more than
nothing

that's what this tail is all about

and, if you haven't been there
you could never know
don't even think about going there
it's never what it seems

6

night smashes hard
against the dripping illusion
of hollywood nothingness
and I go out onto the streets—AGAIN

seeking a cure—which is non-existent
seeking the miracles—which never
seem to come
but, still I go

we walk down cahuenga B-L-V-D
intensions on *the burgundy room*

we, ken-dog, and I go inside
small, dark, smoky

like, you know, the style
all the places depicted
in all those 1940 hollywood movies

back when smoking was cool
back before it was revealed the smoke
KILLED you dead
back before it was told the tobacco
companies
were messing with nicotine levels
        to addict faster
        to suck you in
        to kill you harder

            die—in a deathful way

speaking of. . .

it was dead inside
dead, in the way only hollywood
        dead could be
filled to the brim with neo-hip
        hollywood types

        goatees
        dudes, hair shaved tight
        chicks—died platinum blonde
        retro bell bottoms

        we walk out

now I'm hang'n tonight with this guy
met him maybe five years back
doing a film
when I was an evil drug dealing—killer
        co-star
he was an asian drug kingpin

back in the days when I was a bad actor
but, I got a lot of roles

back when my long hair
was considered cool
back when my very baggy suits
for a moment
were the trend

        back then...

now, a relative good actor
and…
anyway, me and he/he and me—we
went on
made a few films together
got some not bad reviews
but made no money

he's got a job
me, I still make the movies

we walk across the streets
jay-walk cahuenga B-L-V-D
we notice people walking down
        the alley way-backside
"let's go take a look."

we walk past a bum
like a guardian into the abyss-full
realms
of the deathful nothing
posted at the side of empty parking lot
guarding nothing but his lifeless life
guarding the realms which only too few
could ever experience
guarding, as if it all matter
but, it doesn't

we walk

past where the lights fade to a dull
glow

18

past where there are any other people

desolate—cold—old—dying hollywood

    sounds almost poetic
    believe me, it's not

up inside another smoky bar
people crowd together
way too much
way too much for each other

any other place
any other time
they would never even want
to be so close
    to the equally hollywood stylish
    equally hollywood trendy
        goatees
        cigarettes
        dr. martin boots

grabbed a couple budweiser from the
bar maid
nothing really left to do
nothing, for sure, left to lose

bam! one hit

mine, in was gone
pass me another, if you please

in my left ear

I'm hearing the meaningless chatter
of the meaningless masses
in my right ear
a dude way to close
exclaims to his friend,
"if you carry a gun, that only means
you are waiting for the time to kill
someone."

waiting, I think
as if it hasn't already happened
a time, no two, no three...
I mean fuck,
this is L.A.

I laugh to myself

me, I'm strapped
I look down at my ankle
a glock held tight

I look over at my partner
his waistline
underneath his coat
glock
        we both have gats

a bullet and the city
hollywood
and this one's got your name on it
mutha' fucker
right between the eyes

finish our beers
we leave
this bar
way too cool for us.

7

I remember this one time
I'd been sitting on a gram or three
      of *caine*
I'd do a solo line here/a solo line there
but, this night—saturday night
alone, too alone
no one to call/no one who wanted to
hear it

I banged down a line
nostril right
banged down a line
nostril left
times ten, fifteen, twenty—I don't
know...
      I don't remember

I was ON/I was wired

OUT—called
but where was out?

solo
is always so god damned HARD

anyway, I got in my jeep—top off
dead of winter
     california winter
wearing this long, east coast style coat
I own
its brown—kinda

I drove...
drove south down *pacific coast
highway*
deep into the reaches of long beach
the LBC
where the cambodian whores exist
if you know where to find 'em
where the *gang bangers* dwell

maximum violence

>I've always preferred the seedy
>the low
>the rundown
>somehow I feel safer there

anyway, back to the storyline at hand...

wired on the *caine*
living the heaven only cocaine
>can make you feel

though my world had been falling down
around me
no one/no thing/no care

BAM—I was cured
Cocaine—the cure

I once had this chick

my once-upon-a-time, main L.A. babe
fucked up head, maximum

we lined up one day
"shit, why don't they make this stuff
legal," she said
"it would cure a lot of depressed
people."
"no shit... and, addict a lot more," I
added

> a reason for larceny
> a reason for violence
> a reason to kill

but, that was then,
a long time ago
a time long before this...

but me, I drove through the gutters
caine pounding in my brain
"IT'S ALL GOING TO BE OKAY,
ALRIGHT."
instant cure, at the hands of a drug
so I hit the seedy side/the dark side
where all the dweller of the night
embrace their unique brand of
mysticism

I drive/I see

a cambodian darling
pacing the pathways of the night

    I drive by once
    she looks
    I drive by twice
    she smiles
    I drive by a third time
    she gets in

now, I've watched *cops* on T.V.
    way too many times
and where the fuck there are hookers
for $20.00
damned if I will ever find out

this is L.A., long beach, south of
hollywood
and a *scag-hoe*
walking the street

wants $100.00 minimum
to clean my plumbing

    seemed like a fair price to pay...

the night time sky looked fine
as I stared up from my jeep
I stared into the sky
saw the few remaining stars

that the L.A./LBC smog lets you see

I lay back
I look up
my back laying on my reclined seat
she was on top of me
in control of the action
my mind on cuming/on her/on this
moment
on hoping the cops/or some *bangers*
don't drive by
and interrupt our session

occasionally
I glanced at her
pretty
I could have loved her
once upon a time
now
her life/like mine
way to gone to ever be known
way too much knowledge
of the kind that no one else can know
no one else can understand

    I call it
    the enlightenment of the street
    it takes a long time to find
    a lot longer to know
    but once you know

you know
and it is something
so few cold ever grasp.

our enlightenment met with our merged
bodies
my dick planted deeply into her
on the streets of the late night

LBC

8

walking through a midnight parking lot
out of the corner of my eye
I see this girl
passing
the other way

       she
       she sees me

       she stares
       I know those eyes

now, what has it been
ten years?
no, more like fifteen

a one time dream
a one time lover
of a one time fantasy

once upon a one time
that I thought would last forever

should have/could have/did not

in thinking back
I am so glad
I walked when I walked
back then
way back then

psycho bitch
you know the one
every poet writes about her

but hot
she was hot

dyed black hair
even though
        her hair was naturally black
dyed black heart
bright red lips
chinese eyes
could fuck
like there was no tomorrow

I see her
I see her see me

I know
I remember
but, I keep my walk
walking on

that night/then
I go and get my drink on
waltz back to my ride
I drive
having forgotten the vision
of what I had seen/her

a couple of hours the previous

I drive
      hop the freeway
      405 south

I drive
I get off
a little hold up in one lane

the one lane
over to my right

up next to me
pulls a car
a car I had never seen before
I glance
another glance
a third glance out of
the corner of my eyes

like the one before
earlier that evening

I glance
and there she is
a vision of remembrance
remembrance for the second time

she has followed me

tried to follow me home
tried to find out where I live
discover what went wrong
try to live the love again
try to haunt my dreams
one more time

ten
no fifteen
fifteen years later

I look
I see

I take the opportunity
I jam off
turn left
when I want to turn right

run
as she is tied up
tied in the one-lane
that has traffic problems

I drive
I think
I realize
people never change

not her/not I

not the what should have been
that moment
hers and mine
that span two years

but, her silent chase
it has left me with the question
a remembrance
of what should never have been
but was

I question
should I just have smiled
said, "hi."
and reentered the nightmare

9

she was a beautiful little creature
nisei
japanese princess

she earned her wage
playing mini-mouse
over disneyland way

we met
when I was casting a movie
    at a coffee house
over on beverly blvd.
    west hollywood

long black hair
eyes that kissed the night
and she loved me

me—too
I fell in love with her

we did
what you do in hollywood
    when love is fresh
    when love is new

we got in on guest-lists
saw friends who were in bad-bands
    playing bad music
    dreaming of stardom

we made love on the beaches
in the back seats of cars

didn't need to
didn't have to
it is/was
just the perfection of the moment
      the lost space in time
      when the new love
      is all that matters
      when the new love is the promise
      that will take you away
      from the night

one day
over at a friend's music shop
a shop where I get my guitars
made/tuned up
a guy
a bass player that I knew
made his wage playing
on one of disneyland's stages
"you know her?"
"you're going out with her?"
"man, I have had fantasies about that
girl!"

      and life it is a fantasy
      a fantasy
      you have to live

live for life
for it is all that we have
for it is all that we know

live to live
because what else is there

the girl
I gave her a part in a movie

her first starring role
I gave her a part
but there was the problem
I was working with a guy on the film
letting him ride my wave
he claimed/pretended
to be my friend
she had the chance to talk to him
that was my mistake

she asked the wrong questions
to the wrong guy

he told her I was a vampire
a creature who prowled the streets
deeply hidden in the night

a touch/a kiss
drink the blood
take what any woman has to give me

then I would be gone
lost into the night
        the girl left holding her heart
        in her hand

true to some/if not many degrees
but it is all how the stories are told

the girl got scared
she ran away

lost
was that chance to see what happened

and I will never know
what it may have equaled
stolen by the words
the hidden jealousies
of a so-called friend
        and you never what you never
know

years later
I sat near the beach
eating lunch
with this so-called friend

he tells me
his life ended

when I stopped
        making movies with him

when I stopped
        inviting him along for the ride

I smile
I remembered
I go home
and write these words
about a part of my life ended
when I was betrayed

a part of my life
that was not allowed to play out
        and I will never know
        what I will never know

so lost
so long ago

that girl
in a dream
I remember how
we made love
on a nighttime beach

10

venchenzo calls me up
about twelve
in the noon o'clock
"hey, what's up, man?"
"you want to go and waste some more
money and some more time."
"noth'n to lose but my life, my man.
I'm there."

so, I hit over to his crib
down venice way

early, on an early start
"yeah, we may as well drink all day," I
said

but the life time
turns into the night time
and I can't help but wonder
where the time has gone

yeah, I know
years in asia
years lost in day dreams
equaling little
on the equaling scale
but then,
what does life really equal anyway

venchenzo and me
we were doing
        this same thing a decade back

he questions our, "why"

"we never got old," I answer
"never had a reason to."
"never had kids."
"never had house payments."
"never had some chick
telling us we had to stop behaving this
way."

all good or bad
I just know
your call

post a basketball game on the T.V.
post a dozen beers each
post a bottle of the grape, maybe two
time to take life to the life-line
time to hit the streets

Hollywood
        the rainbow

back when venchenzo and I were punks
PUNKS in the stylistic side of the word
that place used to be a joke
then came the re-made/re-do

late 1980's heavy metal craze
and. . .
for what ever fool's reason
we went—THERE—upon occasion
I guess nothing better to do

now, deep in the 1990's
lost in a city with no direction
a jungle of purpose with no style

every now and then
we dig *the rainbow* out of the places
we every-time claim
"NEVER AGAIN"

inside on a neon filled saturday night
the dudes with hair still teased
up way too high
the chicks with skin tight vinyl pants
and spike heels

I just don't understand
how people can get lost
in an era
which *ain't never com'n back*

inside
post a pound down of a dozen drinks
        or so
the dance floor is pick'n up

we strut our bad self's down there
venchenzo and I

post your basic eye contact
I move in and on
with this six month(s) here
japanese
out-a-tokyo chick

oh yeah, did I mention
a lot of japanese chicks tend to hang
there
you know, the japanese *thAng* for
americans
rock n' roll and all...

as mentioned, I move in and on
to this female
of a not even nearly nearing
semi fine babe
who dances, like all asian chicks seem
to do
badly, and into the mirror

personally, I don't get it
it's kinda like jack'n off, I guess
but, I just don't want to watch myself
dance
hell, or watch myself jack off
for that matter...

so, I get my grove on with her
slide in between the mirror and her-self

just for the record
it is, however, god damned hard
to get your rhythm on
to some late 1980's head bang'n band

anyway...

venchenzo tries to move in
on her straight out of the tokyo
back street friend
he slices his soul-full self up tight on
her
way too tight, I guess
she wasn't ready to play
she pushes him back
"fuck you," he yells
punches a wall
walks off and gets another drink

me, no passion with a purpose
the chick apparently dig'n my scene
I move on/in/closer/tighter

the dancing fades into the never-never
I look over
venchenzo relocated himself
he's got this black chick

tight up against the wall
he's sliding up and down her form

she's obviously more responsive
he's got a drink in one hand
her ass in the other
moving with all his best
        white boy/soul-full moves

venchenzo and I
kinda strange, I guess
like my shrink tells me
white on the out side
but inside I see myself as black

I don't know
I guess my formative years
growing up on the wrong side of the
tracks
down south-central L.A. way
        the only white boy
        in an all black school

first girl I slapped lips with
black
I was five years old

I still remember the feeling
of her buck teeth
plastered against my mouth

I move/venchenzo moves

all hoping for something more than
nothing
a touch/a feel/a kiss/a fuck

venchenzo's dancing left of me
I look
I guess the drink called him out
more than the chick
    without a word
    he leaves her dancing solo
    she watches his movement
    as he walks from the dance floor

    she doesn't know what to do

he does that
when he needs a drink
he just picks up and walks away
no word/no sound/no look

    she
    the girl
    the sweet soul sister
    retreats with her solo moves
    up against the wall

    she sways
    as the hard rock pounds

me, I'm still locked up with the hoped
for
promised passion
dancing

when up walks
these two dudes
way longed haired with bangs
cowboy boots, tight black pants,
leather jackets
        you know the type
        losers...

they, especially this one
apparently knows my latched into
fresh off the boat
japanese chick
        he leans in
        he talks to her

now, this goes on for a moment or three
I scan my mind
there is a couple of ways
I could handle this situation
        because I am not liking
        what I see

        one, bail

        no, can't do that

        two, go and move with
        venchenzo's black soul sister
        show the chick, I just don't care

        no, can't do that either
        can't *dis* my friend

option three
which I choose

I reach my arm out
wrap it around the guy's neck
I pull him in tight to me
all smiles, I say,
"if you don't get the fuck out of here
immediately
       I am going to take your fuck'n
       ass out of the picture right here,
       right now."

I let go
I smile at him
I smile at the girl
he looks at me
scared
and leaves

I dance on

post, the previous
venchenzo reemerges
new drink in his hand
walks up to the black chick
begins to move as if he had never left
the night goes on
we, venchenzo and me, drive home --
solo
a telephone number in my pocket
a telephone number
which I will never call

11

I was teaching this university class
on filmmaking

    class overloaded

with egos
with wanta be filmmakers
with dykes
with idiots
with idiot dykes
with exchange students
    wanting only a visa
    to live close to
    hollywood

with a porn filmmaker
armenian *gangsta*

    why he even took the class
    it was a surprise
    to me

but the last night of said class
he invites me out
we go to *down hollywood*
strip club way

we hit *jumbo's*
old school hollywood
we hit *cheetas*
new school hollywood

now
if I have any advice to give you
it would be
to go out to a strip club
with an armenia *gangsta*

but post the advice
& back to the story at hand

the night rained
in its rock n' roll visions
as the music pounds
and the girls dance on their poles

these are the nights I have known
way too many times to count

I notice a girl
a dancer
a one time b-movie star
I put her in a movie once
once, a long-long time ago

she dances
no one seems to care
I go up to the stage
a ten dollar bill
s

tuck between my lips
I lick it

  It's just my way. . .

I place it
in front of her

I smile
as I think back to the one time fantasy
the fantasy I had about her
so, so long ago...

now, here she dances
alone on a stage
older, much older
older, like I
and the fantasy
it is all gone

I place the money on the stage
I smile
I turn
I walk away

I was the only one
who cared enough
to toss a dime
         how sad was that?

I didn't see her
the dancer
the one-time b-movie queen
the rest of that night
what I did see
was lap dance after lap dance
paid for by the house
paid for with the sweat of the girls

paid for by a student
from a class
armenia *gangsta*
armenia porn filmmaker
a class I taught
over
university extension way

we congregate back at the table
my student, the girls, and I

"I almost came," he exclaims
"wow, that is serious
        premature ejaculation," I thought

but more importantly
one girl
she was in love

she was jealous of the
gorgeous
blonde
wanta-be
actress
who licked my face
touched my body
and rubbed my dick
for an eternity

        eternity
        in terms of the strip club world

she really should have stayed in idaho

this dancer/this dream

because hollywood
is no place for anybody

all you end up to be is
a stripper/a hooker/a dreamer

      a dreamer
      of dreams that can never be

but, this girl
a dancer
not the dancer
another dancer
she was jealous
she had impatiently
awaited my return
she wanted me
for me
me for her
her for now
now forever

      she was alright in her own way
      do-able, I guess

      long dark hair
      big spanish eyes
      do-able
      for lack of anything better to do

now most people go to strip clubs

believing that they can get laid
but it never happens
at least not for most
strippers are not hooker
at least they are not hookers yet

strippers
are believers
they think that tomorrow
mr. right
is going to walk through that door
mr. right
will come in
and save them from their hell
but for some reason
strippers love me
I guess
they think
I am that mr. right
        how wrong they are
but, I always get the invite
        out/later

but this night/that night
I had my student
he was my age
looked way older
and he was too fucked up to drive

so I got the girls digits
he/my student and I
jumped in his range rover

I drove us down to *sam woo's*
      in chinatown
to get our grub on
then got him back to his *bel aire* pad

4:00 A.M.
I make a telephone call
on the cell
one more mr. right
who is not
one more night with a girl

and I do not even remember her name

welcome to hollywood

12

a night
a night club

venchenzo gets up to hit the head
I lay back in the cut
listing to some new wave pop
from the early 1980s
playing over the sound system
yeah, I was there,
        then

my eyes scan
for any possible signs of promised
passion
a female with a willing glance
        I see nothing
        nothing worth my attention

I look over and see a line forming
at the men's head
the door is open
I see venchenzo sitting on the toilet
        not shitting/just sitting
        he's gone down hard
        on a day
        with just too many flavors of
alcohol

he sits/I watch
I've got his back

waiting for any wanta-be asshole
to break fly with him
give him some shit
give me a reason/a moment
to liven up the night

to go and take somebody/some asshole
out

but, they're all nothing
they wait like fool's
        standing
        waiting
        for a guy sitting on a toilet
        to fucked up to stand up
        I wait for some action
        but there is none

13

a lot of people lie to themselves
tell themselves that it all
     means something
     something as opposed to nothing
     something on the nothing scale

     jobs
     family
     cars
     houses
     credit cards

     payments
     to pay for a something

     me, I prefer to just get drunk

14

the evening begins
as they begin
I hop over to 711
in hermosa
grab a big—bad
super jumbo-sized java
three mini creams
three mini mochas
       additives added

I drive down
the p.c.h.
hit venice
hit venchenzo's

we pop down a dozen
cans of the elixir
hit the night
hit the hollywood
where there is sill
one remaining
gothic underworld club
worth going to

we go
we enter
walk pass the girl
collecting dollars at the door
       I smile
       I wave
       I never pay

inside, it is pounding
pounding, it all its darkness

dark to light
light to night
the secret realm of screams
known only to the knowers

two girls sitting solo
we go and make convo

I mean
no one else was...

they looked far
distant
not in the right place
not in the right space
                of time
                or mind

we talk
we drink
we get further
        fucked up
we go back to venchenzo's crib
back by the venice beach

inside,
my girl

interested
we go into the bathroom

my hand in the pudding
her tongue down my throat
         she is pulling down my zipper

when I hear,
"slut!"
"slut!"
"you're a slut!"

her friend's voice rings out

         obviously venchenzo
         wasn't getting any...

so story told
her friend throws
the major
                 cock
                 block

she
the girl
my girl
says she is sorry
says she will call me in the AM

it turns out
she only lives a few blocks from me

down on the beach
soutbay

the girls they leave
we
venchenzo and I
sit in the absolute
of zero
       we drink
       like only
       true broken friends can do

yes, we are the damned
       two of the damned

       another night
       another dream stolen

I go home
I go to sleep
a call in the AM
the girl wants to pick up
where we left off

but any night illusion
is never worth seeing
in the day
where the effects of the goddess drink
have faded
and what could have been
never came to be

       this is hollywood.

15

we're out
out the door
grab a couple of *two-fours* for the road
we drink 'em *en route*
dance club
no action
we leave
120 miles an hour
my '64 porsche 356 sc
down the freeway
I don't remember why
blacked out
but I do remember the gage
120 miles an hour

they always say you know you're an
alcoholic
when you have black outs
        I've had way too many to count

I think somebody wanted to race me
they lost

we go to a strip club
new vietnamese chick
she does a table dance
she's raw
rubs her bar pussy on my forehead
yeah
we go home
do

what
I can't remember
what
sleep it off
a night to be reassured of the
nothingness

> I did something
> I did someone
> I just don't remember
> who/what

16

friday
traffic
major traffic
on the 405 south bound

my wheels rumble under me
the freeway in need of repair

dead Stop
all Stop
non Stop

the city
people of the city
going somewhere to nowhere
nowhere to nothing

something always ends up equaling
nothing

and, where do I go in this mass of
confusion
me, seeking illusion
obsessing about the obsess-able
dreaming of another desire
another place
another time
anther illusion to allow my body
to fall into
embraced
sucked in

drowned in the love
the lust

and, in the end
that too
will all mean nothing

but the nothing which means something

the nothing which equals something
else

the radio plays songs from the 1980s

the 1980s
a decade ago
a musical era ago
where did it all go

     a decade
     ten years
     a lifetime
     gone, spent, lived, lost

a dream of a memory
the memory of being in some stranger's
arms

     she had dark curly hair
     I do remember that
     a perm, I surmised
     had laughing eyes
     and a body that sucked me in

and I remember her
only for a moment

only as superficially
as a memory can be remembered

it was her, bangkok
a decade ago

and, her memory tosses me into the
wonder
the wonder of why I am here, L.A.
traffic
traffic-jammed

the wonder of why I am not there,
bangkok
where all the dreams are so close at
hand

17

this girl
she asks to be in one of my movies

a fine little
       wonder white bread *thAng*
              out of texas

"I'll take my top off"
       she tells me

I smile
       "you don't have to
             take your top off.
       at least not in the movie."

then we go out
we go to have a drink
we drink a lot
I mean, the girl could drink
kept up with me
round-for-round

she was looking for new meaning
came out here to L.A.
to find just that
me, I was looking for a new lie
another lie in the passion

       where, as it has been for years
       any dream will do

it all came together
her/and I
perfection in the making

    almost perfect
    almost time
    but have you ever meant
    one thing
        yet said another
    words that just did not
        come out right
    I did that
        to her
    over the telephone line

    a joke
        came out like an insult

    I didn't really mean it that way

    so what could have been
        never was/never happened

    I don't know
    maybe it was the gods of destiny
    saving me
        from some cruel
        and heartless fate
    maybe it was just payback
        payback for all the babes

        I walked away from
        left before

anything
was ever allowed
to happen

but here it is
for the memory
here it is
for the chance

here it is
for what never happened
here it is
for the dream
that should have been lived

but now it is all too late
I wish
I remembered her name

18

I'm forty-four years old
I have a twenty year old
girl friend

twenty years old
and she is in love with me

I try to remember
call up from the dark ages
recapture
how it feels
to be in love
at twenty

I can think about it
it is like an old forgotten movie

> distant
> faded
> remembered
> but gone

love
infatuation
that totality of creation

that
all that matters
dream

that fantasy
of forever

I think
I remember
but
I cannot feel that way anymore
    how sad is that?

I have long wanted to
dive back in
dream the dreams
of my youth
recapture
what was taken
what is gone/what is lost

hold on to the dream
for just one more session

       that flame
       that got blown out
           somewhere/sometime

       when
       I do not know
       but gone
       it is gone

       can it be relighted?

so again
I am cast off to the dream

a new dream to feel

I am forty-four
I have a twenty year old
girlfriend

        twenty years old
        and she is in love with me

19

I have one babe
  a hot
  little latina lover

  young
  she is very young

she waits at home
waits by the telephone
waits for me to call

she begs me
to take her out

  out and away
  but she has to be home by ten
  she has curfew

I have another babe
tall and lean
from the right
side of the tracks

  rich/beijing

I sit here
in a coffee house
santa monica
waiting

waiting
to forget
the promise of passion

waiting
to forget the dream

waiting
to lose the desire

waiting
for the choice to come

I try to forget
that I have a desire
but, I can not
the choice is made
I go to my young
latina love

20

fading off into the distance
I look
I walk away

      gone
      distant
      removed
      never to be seen again

      fading...

I sit/I wonder
how many times that has happened
that perfect vision/that perfect girl

      our eyes meet
      we like what we see

      I like her/she likes me

      we smile
          we think
              we wonder

      how to make contact
          but then the time is gone

      she walks/I walk

      our moment of chance is gone
      separated for eternity

the moment
the look

the lost of possible love
the loss of probable lust
it is lost
to the possibility of eternity
        forever

        lost/gone

        left only to the words
        written upon a page

the only trace
of a memory
a memory of what
should have/could have
happened

21

I guess it is the curse of age

      time ticking
      time watching
      hating to waste even one moment

I guess it is the curse of age
wanting all moments
      to equal something more

      be more

but this moment
this time
can only be lost

this hour of wanting
can never be repaired

      funny
      how many hours of my life
      have been spent
      sitting
      speaking of the illusion
      writing of the living

      living a life
      that so few have chosen to know

        most
        want homes

want families
want the promise
            of a promise

thanks
but no thanks

not for me
thank you very much
no thanks

            seeking the dream
            holding onto the lies

            and the female liars
            they always lie

just like life
just like the promises
of the promised

those who hold onto faith

            belief
            the church
            the illusion of forever
            in heaven
            as long as they
            follow the rules on earth

rules
who made those rules up anyway

why are we supposed to want
all the zero

all that promised nothing

     heartache
     work
     humiliation
     bowing to the needs
      and desires
     of others

why is that supposed to be so good?

a dream of a night
waiting to happen

a moment lived
in all of its illusion

     a kiss
     hello

     a kiss
     goodbye

     at least it was
     a moment/a life

     lived...

22

sweet little/sweet *thAng*
lives in *the val*
the val via L.A. via taipei

sweet
with an edge

      a porno edge
      wants to do porno style things

      looks can be deceiving...

short
little
short hair
tiny

asks me,
"what kind of girl do I look for?"
"oh, you'll do just fine," I answer

fine she does/fine she is
a moment/moment(s)
cast to the darkness of eternity
cast to the suchness of reason
giving me a moment to believe
      if only for a moment

      a moment is just fine with me

we go out
hit a bar
here or there
down by the beach

she drives us there
has this very expensive
european sport car

"let's put the top down.'

drive and drink
I've done it so many times before

looking   for   something/lost   in   the
nothing

      the drink
      the girl
      the beach
      the wind blowing through
      my hair

drink done
we're fucked up
we closed out that bad little bar

drink done
love to be made
we walk
hand-in-hand
down to the water

drink done
we make love in the sand

     perfect like
         all perfect loves should be
     lived for a moment
     but remembered for a lifetime

we did make some serious love
     down on the sand

3:00 A.M
maybe 4:00
I'm wired/not tired
the pantry
got to get my eats on

so we drive downtown
among the hallowed/the hollowed
the lost to the night

     how many times
     for how many years
     have I gotten my grub on
     here/there
     deep in the realms of the night

her
not like me
she sleeps
sprawled across the table

the waiter laughs
I laugh at him
laughing at me
laughing at her

       a perfect moment
       in a perfect paradise

after the eats
she goes home/I go home
I see the sun rise behind me
as it illuminates the ocean

framing/outlining
my home
       as I drive up

evening, next
see her again
she states
"I'm sore. you are so big."

I smile as I walk away
she is so small
it could have been one of those things
one of those things
that you dream about
one of those things
that last forever

but
it was not

for when so much perfection is lived
in so short a time
all that can occur
is down hill from here/from there

I saw her
later

she questioned,
"why'd you break up with me?"

"I didn't break up with you.
        I just didn't want to damage the
        perfection."

        let the perfection
        the memory of the perfection(s)

                last a lifetime

About the Author

Scott Shaw is a prolific poet, author, actor, photographer, musician, and filmmaker.

Shaw was born and spent his formative years in Hollywood, California and has since spent years of his life living in various geographical locations throughout Asia. His poetry and literary fiction were first published in literary journals in the late 1970s. He continued forward to have several works of poetry and literature published in book form during the 1980s. As the 1990s dawned, Shaw's writings began to be embraced in Spiritual and Martial Art circles. From this, he has authored a number of books on Zen Buddhism, Yoga, and the Martial Arts published by large publishing houses.

Scott Shaw's
Books-In-Print include:

The Little Book of Yoga Breathing
Nirvana in a Nutshell
About Peace:
        108 Ways to Be at Peace When
        Things Are Out of Control
Zen O'clock: Time To Be
The Tao of Self Defense
Samurai Zen
The Ki Process: Korean Secrets
        for Cultivating Dynamic Energy
The Warrior is Silent:
        Martial Arts and the Spiritual Path
Hapkido:
        The Korean Art of Self Defense
Hapkido: Essays on Self-Defense
Taekwondo Basics
Advanced Taekwondo
Chi Kung For Beginners
Mastering Health:
        The A to Z of Chi Kung
Cambodia Refugees
        in Long Beach, California
China Deep
Essence: The Zen of Everything
Shanghai Whispers/Shanghai Screams
Shattered Thoughts
Junk: The Back Streets of Bangkok
The Passionate Kiss of Illusion
TKO: Lost Nights in Tokyo
Bangkok and the Nights of Drunken Stupor

No Kisses for the Sinner
Scream: Southeast Asia and the Dream
Suicide Slowly
Zen Buddhism: The Pathway to Nirvana,
Zen: Tales from the Journey
Zen in the Blink of an Eye
Yoga: A Spiritual Guidebook
Marguerite Duras and Charles Bukowski:
      The Yin and Yang
            of Modern Erotic Literature